50 Cozy Fall Recipes

By: Kelly Johnson

Table of Contents

- Butternut Squash Soup
- Pumpkin Chili
- Apple Crisp
- Sweet Potato Casserole
- Roasted Root Vegetables
- Chicken Pot Pie
- Butternut Squash Risotto
- Caramelized Onion and Mushroom Gravy
- Cinnamon Rolls
- Baked Apple Cider Donuts
- Pumpkin Bread
- Roasted Brussels Sprouts with Bacon
- Maple Pecan Pie
- Beef Stew
- Stuffed Acorn Squash
- Butternut Squash Mac and Cheese
- Warm Apple Pie
- Cranberry Sauce
- Spaghetti Squash with Parmesan
- Pear and Gorgonzola Salad
- Mushroom and Spinach Lasagna
- Harvest Grain Salad
- Spicy Roasted Pumpkin Seeds
- Pumpkin Spice Latte
- Maple Roasted Carrots
- Pecan Crusted Salmon
- Apple Cider Chicken
- Spiced Pumpkin Soup
- Maple Apple Pork Chops
- Slow Cooker Potato Leek Soup
- Fall Vegetable Stir-Fry
- Roasted Squash and Beet Salad
- Apple and Walnut Salad
- Pumpkin Alfredo Pasta
- Autumn Shepherd's Pie

- Grilled Cheese with Caramelized Onions
- Baked Brie with Cranberry Chutney
- Honey Roasted Sweet Potatoes
- Pumpkin Pie Smoothie
- Cinnamon Baked Apples
- Spiced Mulled Wine
- Chai-Spiced Hot Chocolate
- Baked Pumpkin French Toast
- Squash and Kale Salad
- Cinnamon Sugar Roasted Almonds
- Roasted Apple and Squash Soup
- Pumpkin Risotto
- Caramel Apple Cheesecake Bars
- Slow Cooker Beef and Barley Soup
- Roasted Chestnuts

Butternut Squash Soup

Ingredients:

- 1 medium butternut squash, peeled, seeded, and chopped
- 1 tablespoon olive oil
- 1 medium onion, chopped
- 2 cloves garlic, minced
- 4 cups vegetable broth
- 1/2 cup coconut milk (or heavy cream)
- Salt and pepper to taste
- 1/2 teaspoon ground nutmeg
- 1/2 teaspoon ground cinnamon
- Fresh parsley or thyme for garnish (optional)

Instructions:

1. Heat olive oil in a large pot over medium heat. Add the chopped onion and garlic, sautéing until softened (about 5 minutes).
2. Add the chopped butternut squash, vegetable broth, cinnamon, nutmeg, salt, and pepper. Bring to a boil, then reduce the heat and simmer for 20-25 minutes, until the squash is tender.
3. Use an immersion blender or regular blender to purée the soup until smooth.
4. Stir in the coconut milk or heavy cream for extra creaminess.
5. Garnish with fresh parsley or thyme if desired, and serve warm.

Pumpkin Chili

Ingredients:

- 1 tablespoon olive oil
- 1 onion, chopped
- 1 bell pepper, chopped
- 2 cloves garlic, minced
- 1 can (15 oz) pumpkin puree
- 1 can (15 oz) diced tomatoes
- 1 can (15 oz) kidney beans, drained and rinsed
- 1 can (15 oz) black beans, drained and rinsed
- 2 tablespoons chili powder
- 1 teaspoon cumin
- 1/2 teaspoon smoked paprika
- Salt and pepper to taste
- 2 cups vegetable broth
- 1/4 cup chopped fresh cilantro (optional)

Instructions:

1. Heat olive oil in a large pot over medium heat. Add the onion, bell pepper, and garlic. Sauté for 5-7 minutes until softened.
2. Add the pumpkin puree, diced tomatoes, beans, chili powder, cumin, smoked paprika, salt, and pepper. Stir to combine.
3. Pour in the vegetable broth and bring to a boil. Reduce the heat and simmer for 20-25 minutes, stirring occasionally.
4. Taste and adjust seasoning as needed.
5. Garnish with chopped cilantro and serve warm.

Apple Crisp

Ingredients:

- 6 medium apples, peeled, cored, and sliced
- 1 tablespoon lemon juice
- 1/2 cup granulated sugar
- 1/2 teaspoon ground cinnamon
- 1/4 teaspoon ground nutmeg
- 1/2 cup old-fashioned rolled oats
- 1/4 cup all-purpose flour
- 1/4 cup packed brown sugar
- 1/4 cup unsalted butter, cold and cubed
- A pinch of salt

Instructions:

1. Preheat the oven to 350°F (175°C). Grease a 9-inch baking dish.
2. Toss the sliced apples with lemon juice, granulated sugar, cinnamon, and nutmeg. Spread the apples evenly in the prepared baking dish.
3. In a separate bowl, combine the oats, flour, brown sugar, and a pinch of salt.
4. Cut in the cold butter using a pastry cutter or your fingers until the mixture resembles coarse crumbs.
5. Sprinkle the oat mixture over the apples.
6. Bake for 40-45 minutes, until the topping is golden brown and the apples are tender.
7. Serve warm with a scoop of vanilla ice cream if desired.

Sweet Potato Casserole

Ingredients:

- 4 medium sweet potatoes, peeled and cubed
- 1/4 cup unsalted butter
- 1/2 cup brown sugar, packed
- 1/2 teaspoon cinnamon
- 1/4 teaspoon nutmeg
- 1 teaspoon vanilla extract
- 1/4 teaspoon salt
- 1/2 cup mini marshmallows (optional)

Instructions:

1. Preheat the oven to 375°F (190°C). Grease a 9x13-inch baking dish.
2. Boil the sweet potato cubes in a large pot of salted water for 10-12 minutes until tender.
3. Drain the sweet potatoes and return them to the pot. Mash them with butter, brown sugar, cinnamon, nutmeg, vanilla, and salt until smooth.
4. Transfer the mashed sweet potatoes to the prepared baking dish and smooth the top.
5. (Optional) Top with mini marshmallows if you like a sweet, gooey topping.
6. Bake for 25-30 minutes, or until the top is golden brown and the marshmallows are toasted.
7. Serve warm.

Roasted Root Vegetables

Ingredients:

- 2 large carrots, peeled and cut into sticks
- 2 medium parsnips, peeled and cut into sticks
- 1 medium sweet potato, peeled and cubed
- 1 tablespoon olive oil
- 1 teaspoon dried thyme
- 1 teaspoon dried rosemary
- Salt and pepper to taste
- 2 cloves garlic, minced

Instructions:

1. Preheat the oven to 400°F (200°C). Line a baking sheet with parchment paper.
2. In a large bowl, toss the carrots, parsnips, and sweet potato with olive oil, thyme, rosemary, garlic, salt, and pepper.
3. Spread the vegetables in an even layer on the baking sheet.
4. Roast for 25-30 minutes, or until the vegetables are tender and lightly browned, stirring halfway through.
5. Serve warm as a side dish.

Chicken Pot Pie

Ingredients:

- 2 tablespoons unsalted butter
- 1 small onion, chopped
- 1 cup carrots, diced
- 1 cup frozen peas
- 2 cups cooked, shredded chicken
- 1/3 cup all-purpose flour
- 2 cups chicken broth
- 1 cup milk
- Salt and pepper to taste
- 1/2 teaspoon dried thyme
- 1 sheet frozen pie crust (or homemade)

Instructions:

1. Preheat the oven to 375°F (190°C). Grease a 9-inch pie dish.
2. In a large saucepan, melt the butter over medium heat. Add the onion and carrots and sauté until softened (about 5 minutes).
3. Stir in the flour and cook for 1-2 minutes, then slowly add the chicken broth and milk, stirring constantly.
4. Bring the mixture to a simmer and cook for 5-7 minutes, until thickened.
5. Stir in the peas, shredded chicken, salt, pepper, and thyme.
6. Pour the mixture into the prepared pie dish. Cover with the pie crust and crimp the edges to seal.
7. Cut a few slits in the top of the crust to allow steam to escape.
8. Bake for 30-35 minutes, or until the crust is golden brown.
9. Let the pie cool for a few minutes before serving.

Butternut Squash Risotto

Ingredients:

- 1 medium butternut squash, peeled and cubed
- 1 tablespoon olive oil
- 1 medium onion, chopped
- 2 cloves garlic, minced
- 1 1/2 cups Arborio rice
- 4 cups vegetable broth
- 1/2 cup white wine
- 1/2 cup grated Parmesan cheese
- Salt and pepper to taste
- Fresh parsley for garnish (optional)

Instructions:

1. Preheat the oven to 400°F (200°C). Toss the butternut squash cubes with olive oil, salt, and pepper. Roast for 20-25 minutes, until tender and golden.
2. In a large saucepan, heat olive oil over medium heat. Add the onion and garlic and sauté until softened (about 5 minutes).
3. Stir in the Arborio rice and cook for 1-2 minutes, toasting the rice slightly.
4. Add the white wine and cook until absorbed, then begin adding the vegetable broth, one ladle at a time, stirring constantly. Wait until the liquid is absorbed before adding more broth.
5. Continue adding broth and stirring until the rice is creamy and tender (about 18-20 minutes).
6. Stir in the roasted butternut squash and Parmesan cheese.
7. Adjust seasoning with salt and pepper. Garnish with fresh parsley if desired.
8. Serve warm.

Caramelized Onion and Mushroom Gravy

Ingredients:

- 2 tablespoons unsalted butter
- 1 large onion, thinly sliced
- 1 cup mushrooms, sliced
- 2 cups vegetable broth
- 1 tablespoon all-purpose flour
- Salt and pepper to taste
- 1/2 teaspoon thyme

Instructions:

1. In a skillet, melt butter over medium heat. Add the onion and cook, stirring occasionally, for 20-25 minutes until caramelized.
2. Add the mushrooms and cook for another 5-7 minutes, until softened.
3. Stir in the flour and cook for 1-2 minutes, then slowly add the vegetable broth while stirring.
4. Bring to a simmer and cook for 5-7 minutes, until thickened.
5. Season with salt, pepper, and thyme.
6. Serve over mashed potatoes or roasted meats.

Cinnamon Rolls

Ingredients:

- 1 cup warm milk
- 2 1/4 teaspoons active dry yeast
- 1/3 cup granulated sugar
- 1/2 cup unsalted butter, softened
- 1 teaspoon salt
- 2 eggs
- 4 cups all-purpose flour
- 1/2 cup brown sugar, packed
- 2 tablespoons ground cinnamon
- 1/2 cup unsalted butter, melted
- 1 cup powdered sugar
- 1/2 teaspoon vanilla extract
- 1-2 tablespoons milk (for glaze)

Instructions:

1. In a bowl, combine warm milk, yeast, and granulated sugar. Let sit for 5-10 minutes until foamy.
2. Add the butter, salt, eggs, and flour, mixing until a dough forms. Knead for 5-7 minutes until smooth.
3. Place the dough in a greased bowl, cover, and let rise for 1 hour.
4. Preheat the oven to 375°F (190°C). Punch down the dough and roll it out on a floured surface into a rectangle.
5. Brush the dough with melted butter, then sprinkle with brown sugar and cinnamon.
6. Roll the dough tightly and cut into 12 slices. Place in a greased 9x13-inch pan.
7. Bake for 20-25 minutes, until golden brown.
8. While baking, mix the powdered sugar, vanilla, and milk to make the glaze.
9. Drizzle the glaze over the warm cinnamon rolls and serve.

Baked Apple Cider Donuts

Ingredients:

- 2 cups all-purpose flour
- 1/2 teaspoon baking powder
- 1/2 teaspoon baking soda
- 1 teaspoon ground cinnamon
- 1/4 teaspoon ground nutmeg
- 1/2 teaspoon salt
- 1/2 cup granulated sugar
- 1/4 cup brown sugar, packed
- 1 large egg
- 3/4 cup apple cider, reduced to 1/2 cup by simmering
- 1/4 cup unsweetened applesauce
- 1/4 cup milk
- 2 tablespoons unsalted butter, melted
- 1 teaspoon vanilla extract

For the Coating:

- 1/4 cup unsalted butter, melted
- 1/2 cup granulated sugar
- 1 teaspoon ground cinnamon

Instructions:

1. Preheat the oven to 350°F (175°C). Grease a donut pan.
2. In a medium bowl, whisk together the flour, baking powder, baking soda, cinnamon, nutmeg, and salt.
3. In a large bowl, mix together the sugars, egg, apple cider, applesauce, milk, melted butter, and vanilla extract until smooth.
4. Gradually add the dry ingredients to the wet ingredients, stirring until just combined.
5. Spoon the batter into the prepared donut pan, filling each cavity about 3/4 full.
6. Bake for 10-12 minutes, until a toothpick comes out clean.
7. While the donuts are baking, melt the butter for the coating. Mix the sugar and cinnamon in a separate bowl.
8. Once the donuts are done, remove them from the pan and dip each in the melted butter, then roll in the cinnamon-sugar mixture.

9. Serve warm.

Pumpkin Bread

Ingredients:

- 1 3/4 cups all-purpose flour
- 1 teaspoon baking powder
- 1/2 teaspoon baking soda
- 1 teaspoon ground cinnamon
- 1/2 teaspoon ground nutmeg
- 1/4 teaspoon ground ginger
- 1/2 teaspoon salt
- 1 cup canned pumpkin puree
- 1/2 cup granulated sugar
- 1/2 cup packed brown sugar
- 2 large eggs
- 1/2 cup vegetable oil
- 1/4 cup milk
- 1 teaspoon vanilla extract

Instructions:

1. Preheat the oven to 350°F (175°C). Grease and flour a 9x5-inch loaf pan.
2. In a medium bowl, whisk together the flour, baking powder, baking soda, cinnamon, nutmeg, ginger, and salt.
3. In a large bowl, whisk together the pumpkin, sugars, eggs, oil, milk, and vanilla until smooth.
4. Gradually add the dry ingredients to the wet ingredients, mixing until just combined.
5. Pour the batter into the prepared loaf pan and smooth the top.
6. Bake for 60-70 minutes, or until a toothpick comes out clean.
7. Allow the bread to cool before slicing and serving.

Roasted Brussels Sprouts with Bacon

Ingredients:

- 1 pound Brussels sprouts, trimmed and halved
- 4 slices bacon, chopped
- 1 tablespoon olive oil
- Salt and pepper to taste
- 1 tablespoon balsamic vinegar (optional)

Instructions:

1. Preheat the oven to 400°F (200°C).
2. In a large bowl, toss the Brussels sprouts with olive oil, salt, and pepper.
3. Spread them in a single layer on a baking sheet.
4. Scatter the chopped bacon over the Brussels sprouts.
5. Roast for 20-25 minutes, stirring halfway through, until the Brussels sprouts are crispy and the bacon is browned.
6. Drizzle with balsamic vinegar before serving, if desired.

Maple Pecan Pie

Ingredients:

- 1 1/2 cups pecans, chopped
- 1 1/2 cups maple syrup
- 1/2 cup granulated sugar
- 1/2 cup unsalted butter, melted
- 3 large eggs
- 1 teaspoon vanilla extract
- 1 tablespoon all-purpose flour
- 1/4 teaspoon salt
- 1 9-inch pie crust, unbaked

Instructions:

1. Preheat the oven to 350°F (175°C).
2. In a medium bowl, whisk together the maple syrup, sugar, butter, eggs, vanilla extract, flour, and salt until smooth.
3. Stir in the chopped pecans.
4. Pour the filling into the unbaked pie crust.
5. Bake for 45-50 minutes, until the filling is set and the top is golden brown.
6. Let the pie cool before serving.

Beef Stew

Ingredients:

- 2 pounds beef stew meat, cubed
- 1 tablespoon olive oil
- 1 onion, chopped
- 3 cloves garlic, minced
- 4 carrots, peeled and sliced
- 3 potatoes, peeled and cubed
- 1 cup celery, chopped
- 4 cups beef broth
- 1 cup red wine (optional)
- 2 tablespoons tomato paste
- 1 teaspoon dried thyme
- Salt and pepper to taste
- 2 tablespoons flour (for thickening)

Instructions:

1. In a large pot or Dutch oven, heat the olive oil over medium heat.
2. Add the beef stew meat and brown on all sides. Remove the beef and set aside.
3. In the same pot, add the onion and garlic, cooking until softened (about 5 minutes).
4. Stir in the tomato paste, beef broth, red wine, thyme, salt, and pepper.
5. Return the beef to the pot, along with the carrots, potatoes, and celery.
6. Bring to a boil, then reduce the heat and simmer for 1-2 hours, until the beef is tender.
7. In the last 30 minutes, mix the flour with a small amount of water to create a slurry, then stir it into the stew to thicken.
8. Serve warm.

Stuffed Acorn Squash

Ingredients:

- 2 acorn squash, halved and seeded
- 1 tablespoon olive oil
- Salt and pepper to taste
- 1 cup cooked quinoa or rice
- 1/2 cup cranberries, dried
- 1/4 cup walnuts, chopped
- 1 tablespoon maple syrup
- 1 teaspoon cinnamon

Instructions:

1. Preheat the oven to 375°F (190°C).
2. Rub the acorn squash halves with olive oil, salt, and pepper. Place them cut side down on a baking sheet.
3. Roast for 35-40 minutes, until tender.
4. In a bowl, combine the quinoa or rice, cranberries, walnuts, maple syrup, and cinnamon.
5. Once the squash is done, flip them over and stuff the centers with the quinoa mixture.
6. Return to the oven for an additional 10 minutes to heat through.
7. Serve warm.

Butternut Squash Mac and Cheese

Ingredients:

- 1 medium butternut squash, peeled and cubed
- 1 pound elbow macaroni
- 2 tablespoons butter
- 2 tablespoons all-purpose flour
- 2 cups milk
- 1 1/2 cups shredded sharp cheddar cheese
- 1/2 teaspoon ground nutmeg
- Salt and pepper to taste

Instructions:

1. Preheat the oven to 350°F (175°C).
2. Boil the butternut squash cubes in salted water for 10-15 minutes until soft.
3. Cook the macaroni according to package directions.
4. In a large saucepan, melt the butter over medium heat. Stir in the flour and cook for 1-2 minutes.
5. Gradually whisk in the milk and cook until thickened (about 5 minutes).
6. Stir in the cheddar cheese, nutmeg, salt, and pepper.
7. Mash the cooked butternut squash and add it to the cheese sauce, stirring to combine.
8. Toss the cooked macaroni with the sauce, then transfer to a greased baking dish.
9. Bake for 20-25 minutes, until bubbly and golden on top.
10. Serve warm.

Warm Apple Pie

Ingredients:

- 6 medium apples, peeled, cored, and sliced
- 1/2 cup granulated sugar
- 1/2 teaspoon cinnamon
- 1 tablespoon lemon juice
- 1 tablespoon cornstarch
- 1 tablespoon butter, cubed
- 1 prepared pie crust

Instructions:

1. Preheat the oven to 375°F (190°C).
2. Toss the apple slices with sugar, cinnamon, lemon juice, and cornstarch.
3. Roll out the pie dough and place it in a 9-inch pie dish.
4. Pour the apple mixture into the crust and dot with butter.
5. Cover with the top pie crust, trimming and crimping the edges.
6. Cut a few slits in the top to allow steam to escape.
7. Bake for 45-50 minutes, until golden brown.
8. Let cool slightly before serving.

Cranberry Sauce

Ingredients:

- 12 oz fresh or frozen cranberries
- 1 cup granulated sugar
- 1/2 cup water
- 1/2 teaspoon orange zest (optional)

Instructions:

1. In a medium saucepan, combine the cranberries, sugar, and water.
2. Bring to a simmer over medium heat, stirring occasionally.
3. Cook for 10-15 minutes, until the cranberries burst and the sauce thickens.
4. Stir in the orange zest if desired.
5. Let cool before serving.

Spaghetti Squash with Parmesan

Ingredients:

- 1 medium spaghetti squash
- 2 tablespoons olive oil
- Salt and pepper to taste
- 1/2 cup grated Parmesan cheese
- 2 tablespoons fresh parsley, chopped (optional)

Instructions:

1. Preheat the oven to 400°F (200°C).
2. Slice the spaghetti squash in half lengthwise and scoop out the seeds.
3. Drizzle the inside of the squash with olive oil and season with salt and pepper.
4. Place the squash halves cut-side down on a baking sheet and roast for 40-45 minutes, until tender.
5. Once roasted, use a fork to scrape out the strands of squash into a bowl.
6. Toss with grated Parmesan cheese and fresh parsley (if using).
7. Serve warm.

Pear and Gorgonzola Salad

Ingredients:

- 4 cups mixed salad greens
- 2 pears, sliced
- 1/2 cup crumbled Gorgonzola cheese
- 1/4 cup toasted walnuts
- 1/4 cup balsamic vinaigrette

Instructions:

1. In a large salad bowl, toss the mixed greens with the sliced pears, Gorgonzola, and toasted walnuts.
2. Drizzle with balsamic vinaigrette and toss gently to combine.
3. Serve immediately.

Mushroom and Spinach Lasagna

Ingredients:

- 9 lasagna noodles, cooked according to package directions
- 1 tablespoon olive oil
- 1 onion, chopped
- 2 cloves garlic, minced
- 16 oz mushrooms, sliced
- 4 cups fresh spinach
- 15 oz ricotta cheese
- 1 egg
- 2 cups shredded mozzarella cheese
- 1 1/2 cups marinara sauce
- 1/2 teaspoon dried basil
- Salt and pepper to taste

Instructions:

1. Preheat the oven to 375°F (190°C).
2. In a large skillet, heat olive oil over medium heat. Add the onion and garlic, cooking until softened.
3. Add the mushrooms and cook until tender, about 5-7 minutes. Stir in the spinach and cook until wilted.
4. In a medium bowl, mix the ricotta cheese, egg, 1 cup of mozzarella, basil, salt, and pepper.
5. Spread a thin layer of marinara sauce in the bottom of a 9x13-inch baking dish. Layer 3 cooked lasagna noodles on top.
6. Add half of the ricotta mixture, followed by half of the mushroom-spinach mixture. Repeat with another layer of noodles, ricotta, and mushrooms.
7. Top with remaining marinara sauce and mozzarella cheese.
8. Cover with foil and bake for 25 minutes. Remove the foil and bake for an additional 10 minutes, until bubbly and golden.
9. Let it cool slightly before serving.

Harvest Grain Salad

Ingredients:

- 1 cup cooked farro or quinoa
- 1/2 cup roasted sweet potatoes, cubed
- 1/4 cup dried cranberries
- 1/4 cup pumpkin seeds
- 1/4 cup feta cheese, crumbled
- 1 tablespoon olive oil
- 1 tablespoon apple cider vinegar
- 1 teaspoon Dijon mustard
- Salt and pepper to taste

Instructions:

1. In a large bowl, combine the farro or quinoa, roasted sweet potatoes, cranberries, pumpkin seeds, and feta cheese.
2. In a small bowl, whisk together the olive oil, apple cider vinegar, Dijon mustard, salt, and pepper.
3. Drizzle the dressing over the salad and toss to combine.
4. Serve chilled or at room temperature.

Spicy Roasted Pumpkin Seeds

Ingredients:

- 1 cup pumpkin seeds
- 1 tablespoon olive oil
- 1/2 teaspoon smoked paprika
- 1/4 teaspoon cayenne pepper
- Salt to taste

Instructions:

1. Preheat the oven to 350°F (175°C).
2. In a bowl, toss the pumpkin seeds with olive oil, paprika, cayenne pepper, and salt.
3. Spread the seeds in a single layer on a baking sheet.
4. Roast for 10-15 minutes, stirring occasionally, until the seeds are golden and crispy.
5. Let them cool before serving.

Pumpkin Spice Latte

Ingredients:

- 1 cup milk (any variety)
- 1/4 cup pumpkin puree
- 1 tablespoon sugar
- 1/2 teaspoon pumpkin pie spice
- 1 shot espresso or 1/2 cup brewed coffee
- Whipped cream (optional)

Instructions:

1. In a small saucepan, heat the milk, pumpkin puree, sugar, and pumpkin pie spice over medium heat. Whisk to combine.
2. Once the milk mixture is heated through and slightly frothy, remove from heat.
3. Brew the espresso or coffee and pour into a mug.
4. Pour the pumpkin milk mixture over the coffee.
5. Top with whipped cream and additional pumpkin pie spice if desired.
6. Serve warm.

Maple Roasted Carrots

Ingredients:

- 1 pound carrots, peeled and cut into sticks
- 2 tablespoons maple syrup
- 1 tablespoon olive oil
- Salt and pepper to taste

Instructions:

1. Preheat the oven to 400°F (200°C).
2. In a bowl, toss the carrots with maple syrup, olive oil, salt, and pepper.
3. Spread the carrots on a baking sheet in a single layer.
4. Roast for 25-30 minutes, until tender and caramelized, stirring halfway through.
5. Serve warm.

Pecan Crusted Salmon

Ingredients:

- 4 salmon fillets
- 1/2 cup pecans, chopped
- 1/4 cup breadcrumbs
- 2 tablespoons Dijon mustard
- 1 tablespoon honey
- Salt and pepper to taste

Instructions:

1. Preheat the oven to 375°F (190°C).
2. In a small bowl, combine the chopped pecans, breadcrumbs, salt, and pepper.
3. In another small bowl, mix the Dijon mustard and honey.
4. Place the salmon fillets on a baking sheet lined with parchment paper.
5. Brush each fillet with the mustard and honey mixture.
6. Press the pecan mixture onto the top of the salmon fillets.
7. Bake for 15-20 minutes, until the salmon is cooked through and the crust is golden.
8. Serve warm.

Apple Cider Chicken

Ingredients:

- 4 chicken breasts
- 1 tablespoon olive oil
- 1 cup apple cider
- 1/2 cup chicken broth
- 2 tablespoons Dijon mustard
- 2 teaspoons fresh thyme
- 1 tablespoon butter
- Salt and pepper to taste

Instructions:

1. Season the chicken breasts with salt and pepper.
2. Heat olive oil in a large skillet over medium heat. Add chicken breasts and cook until golden brown on both sides, about 5-7 minutes per side.
3. Remove chicken from the skillet and set aside.
4. In the same skillet, add apple cider, chicken broth, Dijon mustard, and thyme. Bring to a simmer, scraping up any browned bits from the bottom of the pan.
5. Return the chicken to the skillet and simmer for 10-15 minutes, until the chicken is cooked through.
6. Remove the chicken and set aside. Stir in butter to the sauce and let it melt.
7. Serve the chicken with the cider sauce spooned over the top.

Spiced Pumpkin Soup

Ingredients:

- 1 can (15 oz) pumpkin puree
- 1 onion, chopped
- 2 cloves garlic, minced
- 2 cups vegetable or chicken broth
- 1/2 cup coconut milk
- 1 teaspoon ground cumin
- 1/2 teaspoon cinnamon
- 1/4 teaspoon ground ginger
- Salt and pepper to taste
- Olive oil for sautéing

Instructions:

1. Heat olive oil in a large pot over medium heat. Add the onion and garlic, cooking until softened, about 5 minutes.
2. Stir in the cumin, cinnamon, and ginger and cook for 1 more minute until fragrant.
3. Add the pumpkin puree, broth, and coconut milk. Stir to combine.
4. Bring the soup to a simmer and cook for 10-15 minutes, stirring occasionally.
5. Season with salt and pepper to taste.
6. Use an immersion blender or regular blender to puree the soup until smooth.
7. Serve warm, garnished with a swirl of coconut milk or roasted pumpkin seeds if desired.

Maple Apple Pork Chops

Ingredients:

- 4 bone-in pork chops
- 2 apples, sliced
- 1/4 cup maple syrup
- 1 tablespoon Dijon mustard
- 1/2 teaspoon ground cinnamon
- 1 tablespoon olive oil
- Salt and pepper to taste

Instructions:

1. Season the pork chops with salt and pepper.
2. Heat olive oil in a large skillet over medium-high heat. Add the pork chops and cook for 4-5 minutes on each side, until browned and cooked through. Remove and set aside.
3. In the same skillet, add the sliced apples, maple syrup, Dijon mustard, and cinnamon. Stir to combine and cook for 5-7 minutes, until the apples are softened.
4. Return the pork chops to the skillet and spoon the maple-apple sauce over them. Cook for another 2-3 minutes to reheat the pork.
5. Serve the pork chops with the maple apple sauce.

Slow Cooker Potato Leek Soup

Ingredients:

- 4 large potatoes, peeled and diced
- 2 leeks, cleaned and sliced
- 4 cups vegetable or chicken broth
- 1/2 cup heavy cream
- 2 cloves garlic, minced
- 1 teaspoon dried thyme
- Salt and pepper to taste
- Olive oil for sautéing

Instructions:

1. In a skillet, heat olive oil over medium heat. Add the leeks and garlic, cooking until softened, about 5 minutes.
2. Transfer the leeks and garlic to the slow cooker. Add the potatoes, broth, thyme, salt, and pepper.
3. Cover and cook on low for 6-8 hours, or on high for 3-4 hours, until the potatoes are tender.
4. Use an immersion blender to puree the soup to your desired consistency.
5. Stir in the heavy cream and adjust seasoning if needed.
6. Serve warm with a sprinkle of fresh herbs or croutons.

Fall Vegetable Stir-Fry

Ingredients:

- 1 cup butternut squash, peeled and diced
- 1 cup Brussels sprouts, halved
- 1 red bell pepper, sliced
- 1/2 cup carrots, sliced
- 1 tablespoon olive oil
- 1 tablespoon soy sauce
- 1 tablespoon maple syrup
- Salt and pepper to taste
- Fresh thyme or rosemary for garnish

Instructions:

1. Heat olive oil in a large skillet or wok over medium-high heat.
2. Add the butternut squash and Brussels sprouts and cook for 5-7 minutes, stirring occasionally.
3. Add the bell pepper and carrots, and cook for another 5-7 minutes, until all the vegetables are tender.
4. Stir in the soy sauce, maple syrup, salt, and pepper. Cook for an additional 2-3 minutes.
5. Serve warm, garnished with fresh thyme or rosemary.

Roasted Squash and Beet Salad

Ingredients:

- 1 small butternut squash, peeled and cubed
- 2 medium beets, peeled and cubed
- 2 tablespoons olive oil
- Salt and pepper to taste
- 4 cups arugula or mixed greens
- 1/4 cup goat cheese, crumbled
- 1/4 cup walnuts, toasted
- Balsamic vinaigrette for drizzling

Instructions:

1. Preheat the oven to 400°F (200°C).
2. Toss the cubed squash and beets with olive oil, salt, and pepper. Spread them on a baking sheet in a single layer.
3. Roast for 30-35 minutes, or until the vegetables are tender and lightly caramelized, stirring halfway through.
4. In a large bowl, toss the roasted squash and beets with arugula, goat cheese, and walnuts.
5. Drizzle with balsamic vinaigrette and serve immediately.

Apple and Walnut Salad

Ingredients:

- 4 cups mixed salad greens
- 1 apple, thinly sliced
- 1/4 cup walnuts, toasted
- 1/4 cup crumbled feta cheese
- 1/4 cup apple cider vinaigrette

Instructions:

1. In a large salad bowl, combine the mixed greens, apple slices, toasted walnuts, and feta cheese.
2. Drizzle with apple cider vinaigrette and toss gently to combine.
3. Serve immediately.

Pumpkin Alfredo Pasta

Ingredients:

- 1 pound pasta (such as fettuccine or penne)
- 1 can (15 oz) pumpkin puree
- 1 cup heavy cream
- 1/2 cup grated Parmesan cheese
- 1 teaspoon ground sage
- 1/4 teaspoon ground nutmeg
- Salt and pepper to taste

Instructions:

1. Cook the pasta according to package instructions and set aside.
2. In a large skillet, heat the pumpkin puree and heavy cream over medium heat. Stir in the Parmesan, sage, nutmeg, salt, and pepper.
3. Cook for 5-7 minutes, until the sauce is heated through and slightly thickened.
4. Toss the cooked pasta in the sauce until well coated.
5. Serve warm, garnished with additional Parmesan cheese if desired.

Autumn Shepherd's Pie

Ingredients:

- 1 pound ground turkey or beef
- 1 onion, chopped
- 2 carrots, diced
- 1 cup frozen peas
- 2 tablespoons tomato paste
- 2 cups beef or vegetable broth
- 4 cups mashed potatoes (prepared ahead of time)
- 2 tablespoons olive oil
- Salt and pepper to taste

Instructions:

1. Preheat the oven to 375°F (190°C).
2. In a large skillet, heat olive oil over medium heat. Add the onion and carrots, cooking until softened, about 5 minutes.
3. Add the ground turkey or beef and cook until browned, about 8 minutes.
4. Stir in the tomato paste and broth. Bring to a simmer and cook for 10-15 minutes, until the mixture thickens. Add the peas and season with salt and pepper.
5. Transfer the meat mixture into a 9x13-inch baking dish.
6. Spread the mashed potatoes on top of the meat mixture.
7. Bake for 25-30 minutes, until the top is golden and bubbly.
8. Serve warm.

Grilled Cheese with Caramelized Onions

Ingredients:

- 4 slices of bread
- 2 tablespoons butter
- 1 large onion, thinly sliced
- 2 teaspoons brown sugar
- 2 tablespoons balsamic vinegar
- 2 cups shredded sharp cheddar cheese
- 1 tablespoon Dijon mustard (optional)
- Salt and pepper to taste

Instructions:

1. In a skillet, melt 1 tablespoon of butter over medium heat. Add the onion and cook, stirring occasionally, until soft and golden brown, about 15 minutes.
2. Add the brown sugar and balsamic vinegar to the onions, stirring to combine. Cook for an additional 5 minutes, until caramelized. Remove from heat.
3. Spread the remaining butter on one side of each slice of bread. Layer the unbuttered side with shredded cheese and a generous amount of caramelized onions.
4. If desired, spread Dijon mustard on the inside of the bread before assembling the sandwich.
5. Heat a skillet over medium heat and grill the sandwiches until golden brown and the cheese is melted, about 3-4 minutes per side.
6. Serve warm.

Baked Brie with Cranberry Chutney

Ingredients:

- 1 wheel of Brie cheese
- 1/2 cup cranberry chutney (store-bought or homemade)
- 1/4 cup chopped walnuts or pecans (optional)
- Fresh thyme for garnish
- Crackers or sliced baguette for serving

Instructions:

1. Preheat the oven to 350°F (175°C).
2. Place the Brie cheese on a baking sheet lined with parchment paper.
3. Bake the Brie for 10-12 minutes, until the cheese is soft and melty but not completely runny.
4. Top the baked Brie with cranberry chutney and sprinkle with nuts (if using).
5. Garnish with fresh thyme and serve with crackers or sliced baguette.

Honey Roasted Sweet Potatoes

Ingredients:

- 4 medium sweet potatoes, peeled and cut into cubes
- 2 tablespoons olive oil
- 2 tablespoons honey
- 1/2 teaspoon cinnamon
- Salt and pepper to taste
- Fresh parsley for garnish

Instructions:

1. Preheat the oven to 400°F (200°C).
2. Toss the sweet potato cubes with olive oil, honey, cinnamon, salt, and pepper.
3. Spread the sweet potatoes in a single layer on a baking sheet.
4. Roast for 25-30 minutes, stirring halfway through, until the sweet potatoes are tender and lightly caramelized.
5. Garnish with fresh parsley before serving.

Pumpkin Pie Smoothie

Ingredients:

- 1/2 cup canned pumpkin puree
- 1/2 cup Greek yogurt
- 1/2 banana
- 1/2 cup almond milk (or any milk of choice)
- 1 tablespoon maple syrup
- 1/2 teaspoon pumpkin pie spice
- Ice cubes (optional)

Instructions:

1. Place all ingredients in a blender.
2. Blend until smooth and creamy, adding ice cubes if desired for a colder, thicker smoothie.
3. Pour into glasses and garnish with a sprinkle of cinnamon or pumpkin pie spice.
4. Serve immediately.

Cinnamon Baked Apples

Ingredients:

- 4 large apples (such as Honeycrisp or Gala)
- 1/4 cup brown sugar
- 1/2 teaspoon ground cinnamon
- 1/4 teaspoon ground nutmeg
- 1/4 cup chopped walnuts or oats (optional)
- 2 tablespoons butter
- 1/4 cup water

Instructions:

1. Preheat the oven to 350°F (175°C).
2. Core the apples, leaving the bottom intact to create a well in the center.
3. In a small bowl, mix the brown sugar, cinnamon, nutmeg, and walnuts or oats (if using).
4. Stuff the apples with the sugar-spice mixture.
5. Place the apples in a baking dish and top each with a tablespoon of butter.
6. Pour water into the bottom of the dish.
7. Bake for 30-40 minutes, until the apples are tender and the filling is bubbling.
8. Serve warm, topped with vanilla ice cream or whipped cream if desired.

Spiced Mulled Wine

Ingredients:

- 1 bottle red wine (750 ml)
- 1/4 cup brandy (optional)
- 1/4 cup honey or sugar (to taste)
- 1 orange, sliced
- 4 whole cloves
- 2 cinnamon sticks
- 2 star anise (optional)
- 1/4 teaspoon ground nutmeg

Instructions:

1. In a large pot, combine the red wine, brandy (if using), honey or sugar, orange slices, cloves, cinnamon sticks, star anise, and nutmeg.
2. Heat over medium heat until warm, but not boiling.
3. Reduce the heat to low and let it simmer for 20-30 minutes to allow the flavors to meld.
4. Strain out the spices and orange slices before serving.
5. Serve warm in mugs with additional orange slices for garnish.

Chai-Spiced Hot Chocolate

Ingredients:

- 2 cups milk (or dairy-free alternative)
- 2 tablespoons cocoa powder
- 2 tablespoons sugar (or to taste)
- 1/2 teaspoon ground cinnamon
- 1/4 teaspoon ground ginger
- 1/4 teaspoon ground cardamom
- 1/4 teaspoon ground cloves
- 1/4 teaspoon ground black pepper
- 1/4 teaspoon vanilla extract
- Whipped cream (optional)

Instructions:

1. In a small pot, whisk together the milk, cocoa powder, sugar, cinnamon, ginger, cardamom, cloves, and black pepper over medium heat.
2. Heat until the mixture is warm and smooth, stirring occasionally.
3. Remove from heat and stir in the vanilla extract.
4. Pour into a mug and top with whipped cream if desired.
5. Serve hot and enjoy.

Baked Pumpkin French Toast

Ingredients:

- 1 loaf of challah or brioche bread, sliced
- 1 can (15 oz) pumpkin puree
- 1/2 cup milk
- 1/4 cup brown sugar
- 1 teaspoon cinnamon
- 1/2 teaspoon nutmeg
- 1/4 teaspoon ground ginger
- 3 large eggs
- 1 teaspoon vanilla extract
- Powdered sugar for dusting

Instructions:

1. Preheat the oven to 375°F (190°C) and grease a 9x13-inch baking dish.
2. Arrange the bread slices in a single layer in the baking dish.
3. In a bowl, whisk together the pumpkin puree, milk, brown sugar, cinnamon, nutmeg, ginger, eggs, and vanilla extract.
4. Pour the pumpkin mixture over the bread, making sure each slice is well coated.
5. Cover the dish with foil and bake for 30-35 minutes. Remove the foil and bake for an additional 10-15 minutes, until the top is golden and the center is set.
6. Dust with powdered sugar before serving.

Squash and Kale Salad

Ingredients:

- 2 cups roasted butternut squash, cubed
- 4 cups kale, chopped
- 1/4 cup red onion, thinly sliced
- 1/4 cup dried cranberries
- 1/4 cup toasted pumpkin seeds
- 1/4 cup feta cheese, crumbled
- 2 tablespoons olive oil
- 1 tablespoon balsamic vinegar
- 1 teaspoon honey
- Salt and pepper to taste

Instructions:

1. In a large bowl, toss the kale with olive oil, balsamic vinegar, honey, salt, and pepper. Massage the kale for 1-2 minutes to soften it.
2. Add the roasted butternut squash, red onion, dried cranberries, pumpkin seeds, and feta cheese.
3. Toss everything together and serve immediately.

Cinnamon Sugar Roasted Almonds

Ingredients:

- 2 cups raw almonds
- 1/4 cup sugar
- 1 tablespoon cinnamon
- 1 tablespoon honey
- 1 tablespoon water
- 1/2 teaspoon vanilla extract
- Pinch of salt

Instructions:

1. Preheat the oven to 350°F (175°C). Line a baking sheet with parchment paper or a silicone mat.
2. In a small bowl, mix the sugar, cinnamon, and salt.
3. In a separate bowl, combine the honey, water, and vanilla extract. Add the almonds and stir to coat evenly.
4. Sprinkle the cinnamon-sugar mixture over the almonds and toss to coat thoroughly.
5. Spread the almonds in a single layer on the prepared baking sheet.
6. Roast for 15-20 minutes, stirring halfway through, until the almonds are golden and fragrant.
7. Allow the almonds to cool completely on the baking sheet before serving.

Roasted Apple and Squash Soup

Ingredients:

- 1 medium butternut squash, peeled, seeded, and cubed
- 2 apples, peeled, cored, and chopped
- 1 medium onion, chopped
- 4 cups vegetable broth
- 2 tablespoons olive oil
- 1 teaspoon ground cinnamon
- 1/2 teaspoon nutmeg
- Salt and pepper to taste
- 1 tablespoon maple syrup (optional)
- Fresh cream for garnish (optional)

Instructions:

1. Preheat the oven to 400°F (200°C). Line a baking sheet with parchment paper.
2. Toss the squash, apples, and onion with olive oil, cinnamon, nutmeg, salt, and pepper. Spread them in an even layer on the baking sheet.
3. Roast for 25-30 minutes until the squash is tender and caramelized.
4. In a large pot, add the roasted vegetables and broth. Bring to a boil, then reduce to a simmer and cook for 10 minutes.
5. Use an immersion blender or regular blender to purée the soup until smooth. Adjust seasoning if necessary.
6. Stir in maple syrup for added sweetness if desired.
7. Serve with a drizzle of cream and a sprinkle of fresh herbs.

Pumpkin Risotto

Ingredients:

- 1 cup Arborio rice
- 1/2 cup canned pumpkin puree
- 4 cups chicken or vegetable broth, kept warm
- 1/2 cup dry white wine
- 1/2 onion, finely chopped
- 2 tablespoons butter
- 1 tablespoon olive oil
- 1/2 cup grated Parmesan cheese
- Salt and pepper to taste
- Fresh sage leaves for garnish (optional)

Instructions:

1. In a large pan, heat the olive oil and butter over medium heat. Add the onion and cook for 5-7 minutes until soft and translucent.
2. Add the Arborio rice and cook for 2-3 minutes, stirring frequently, until the rice is lightly toasted.
3. Pour in the white wine and stir until absorbed.
4. Begin adding the warm broth, one ladle at a time, stirring frequently and allowing the liquid to be absorbed before adding more.
5. After about 10 minutes, stir in the pumpkin puree and continue adding the broth until the rice is tender and creamy (about 20 minutes total).
6. Stir in the Parmesan cheese and season with salt and pepper.
7. Garnish with fresh sage leaves before serving.

Caramel Apple Cheesecake Bars

Ingredients: Crust:

- 1 1/2 cups graham cracker crumbs
- 1/4 cup sugar
- 1/2 cup butter, melted

Cheesecake:

- 16 oz cream cheese, softened
- 1/2 cup sugar
- 1 teaspoon vanilla extract
- 2 large eggs
- 1/2 cup sour cream

Topping:

- 2 medium apples, peeled and diced
- 1 tablespoon butter
- 2 tablespoons brown sugar
- 1/2 teaspoon cinnamon
- 1/4 cup caramel sauce

Instructions:

1. Preheat the oven to 325°F (160°C). Grease a 9x9-inch baking pan and line with parchment paper.
2. For the crust: Mix the graham cracker crumbs, sugar, and melted butter until combined. Press the mixture into the bottom of the pan.
3. For the cheesecake filling: Beat the cream cheese, sugar, and vanilla until smooth. Add the eggs one at a time, beating well after each addition. Stir in the sour cream.
4. Pour the cheesecake batter over the crust and smooth the top.
5. Bake for 35-40 minutes, or until the center is set and the edges are lightly browned. Allow to cool completely.
6. For the topping: In a skillet, melt the butter over medium heat. Add the apples, brown sugar, and cinnamon. Cook for 5-7 minutes until the apples are tender.
7. Spread the caramel apple topping over the cooled cheesecake bars.
8. Drizzle with caramel sauce before serving.

Slow Cooker Beef and Barley Soup

Ingredients:

- 1 lb beef stew meat, cut into cubes
- 1 cup pearl barley
- 4 cups beef broth
- 2 carrots, chopped
- 2 celery stalks, chopped
- 1 medium onion, chopped
- 3 garlic cloves, minced
- 1 teaspoon dried thyme
- 1 bay leaf
- Salt and pepper to taste

Instructions:

1. In the bottom of a slow cooker, combine the beef stew meat, barley, carrots, celery, onion, garlic, thyme, and bay leaf.
2. Pour in the beef broth and stir to combine. Season with salt and pepper.
3. Cover and cook on low for 7-8 hours, or until the beef is tender and the barley is fully cooked.
4. Remove the bay leaf and adjust seasoning if needed.
5. Serve hot with crusty bread on the side.

Roasted Chestnuts

Ingredients:

- 1 lb fresh chestnuts
- Salt, to taste

Instructions:

1. Preheat the oven to 425°F (220°C).
2. Using a sharp knife, score the flat side of each chestnut with an "X" to prevent them from exploding while roasting.
3. Place the chestnuts on a baking sheet in a single layer.
4. Roast in the oven for 20-25 minutes, shaking the pan halfway through.
5. Once roasted, let them cool slightly. Peel off the outer shell and the thin inner skin.
6. Sprinkle with salt and serve warm.

www.ingramcontent.com/pod-product-compliance
Lightning Source LLC
LaVergne TN
LVHW081324060526
838201LV00055B/2453